Hamilton
vs. Jefferson

Curtis Slepian, M.A.

Consultant

Dr. Nicholas Baker
Supervisor of Curriculum and Instruction
Colonial School District, Delaware

Publishing Credits

Rachelle Cracchiolo, M.S.Ed., *Publisher*
Conni Medina, M.A.Ed., *Managing Editor*
Emily R. Smith, M.A.Ed., *Content Director*
Seth Rogers, *Editor*
Robin Erickson, *Senior Graphic Designer*

Image credits: Cover and pp. 1, 4 (left) Niday Picture Library/Alamy Stock Photo, (right) Rembrandt Peale/ZUMA Press/Newscom, (background) Library of Congress Prints and Photographs Division [LC-USZC4-557]; p. 6 and Read and Respond page Library of Congress Prints and Photographs Division [09021562]; p. 5 Library of Congress Prints and Photographs Division [LC-USZC4-9904]; p. 7 Evan Sklar/Alamy Stock Photo; p. 8 Hemis/Alamy Stock Photo; p. 10 Granger, NYC; pp. 11, 17 North Wind Picture Archives; pp. 12–13 Bettmann/Getty Images; pp. 14–15 Thomas Jefferson Foundation; pp. 18, 32 (left) Museum of the American Revolution, (middle) Public Domain, (right) Beyond My Ken; p. 19 Public Domain; p. 20 Library of Congress Prints and Photographs Division [LC-DIG-ppmsca-39743]; p. 21 and back cover National Archives and Records Administration [306462]; pp. 22–23 Metropolitan Museum of Art; p. 23 Ken Welsh/Bridgeman Images; p. 25 Peter Newark Pictures/Bridgeman Images; p. 26 Niday Picture Library/Alamy Stock Photo; p. 28 National Archives and Records Administration [2668821]; p. 29 akg-images/Newscom; all other images from iStock and/or Shutterstock

Teacher Created Materials
5301 Oceanus Drive
Huntington Beach, CA 92649-1030
http://www.tcmpub.com
ISBN 978-1-4258-6354-8
© 2017 Teacher Created Materials, Inc.

Table of Contents

A Tale of Two Men

Thomas Jefferson left a great mark on American history. He served as the third president. He also wrote the Declaration of Independence. His **profound** words about democracy are still repeated and admired.

The work that Alexander Hamilton did for his country is also impressive. He created a financial system that is still being used. He pushed for a strong central government backed by a strong military. His efforts helped to shape the world that Americans live in today.

Alexander Hamilton

Thomas Jefferson

Both men were among the most influential **Founding Fathers**. But, they almost never agreed. These two men had one of the biggest political **rivalries** in history.

We know that they didn't get along, but what was it that each man stood for?

Benjamin Franklin, John Adams, and Jefferson meet to review a draft of the Declaration of Independence.

Face Time

The Treasury Department was planning to replace Hamilton on the $10 bill. Lin-Manuel Miranda's *Hamilton: An American Musical* changed that! Hamilton's face will stay on the bill. Harriet Tubman is expected to appear on the $20 bill instead.

Lasting Legacy

Jefferson's greatest legacy is certainly the Declaration of Independence. "We hold these truths to be self-evident, that all men are created equal, that they are endowed by their Creator with certain unalienable Rights, that among these are Life, Liberty and the pursuit of Happiness." These words are the cornerstone on which the United States was built.

Two Worlds

Not only did Jefferson and Hamilton hold different opinions, but they also lived different kinds of lives. Jefferson was a rich man and lived at Monticello—a huge house that he designed. Not only was he a famous Founding Father, he was also a philosopher, scientist, inventor, and architect.

Displayed inside the house are gadgets Jefferson invented and many objects he collected. Two of these objects stand out: busts of Jefferson and Hamilton. They face each other in the entrance hall. Jefferson said the two heads would be "opposed in death as in life."

Copy Cat

One of Jefferson's favorite gadgets was a copying machine. When he wrote a letter, another pen would duplicate his hand movements. This created a second copy of his letter, which he filed away. Jefferson did not invent the machine, but he did give suggestions to the inventor on how to improve its design.

He Wrote the Guidebook

One of Hamilton's longest-lasting written pieces was a ship-to-ship communication guide. He wrote it in 1790 for the United States Revenue Cutter Service. That group would later become the Coast Guard. The guide was used until 1962.

The Federalist Papers

Elizabeth Hamilton

THE

FEDERALIST:

A COLLECTION

OF

ESSAYS,

WRITTEN IN FAVOUR OF THE

NEW CONSTITUTION,

AS AGREED UPON BY THE FEDERAL CONVENTION, SEPTEMBER 17, 1787.

IN TWO VOLUMES.

VOL. II.

NEW-YORK:

PRINTED AND SOLD BY J. AND A. M'LEAN, No. 41, HANOVER-SQUARE, M,DCC,LXXXVIII.

Unlike Jefferson, Hamilton was never a rich man. As **secretary of the treasury**, he earned $3,500 a year. As a lawyer, he often charged less than he could have. Hamilton had a taste for the finer things in life, but he never had the wealth to back it up. This led to a mountain of **debt**. Hamilton spent most of his free time writing. He wrote a lot, and he wrote quickly. His most famous work appeared in *The Federalist Papers*. These were 85 essays in support of the Constitution. Hamilton wrote 51 of the essays, as many as six of them in one week.

Home Sweet Home

Most of Jefferson's fortune was spent building and furnishing his grand house. He most likely spent more than $100,000 building it. That amount of money would be equal to millions of dollars today. Jefferson owed money when he died, but his **legacy** is rich. His life and words still move people. Half a million people visit Monticello each year.

Hamilton's two-story wooden home, called The Grange, is located in New York City. Built in 1802, the house is much smaller and more modest than Monticello. By the time The Grange was finished, Hamilton was deep in debt. In fact, his wife, Eliza, had to sell the house not long after Hamilton's death to pay off debts. Soon after, she bought the house back and lived in it until 1833. In 1962, The Grange became part of the National Park Service. It is now a national memorial with an exciting history of its own.

The Grange

Monticello

Sweet Tooth

A favorite treat at Monticello was ice cream. Sixty-two wagons full of the dessert were gathered in winter and stored in an icehouse. It's thought that Jefferson wrote the first American recipe for this cool treat.

On the Move

The Grange has been picked up and moved twice. It was first moved in 1889 to avoid being torn down due to street construction. As the city grew around it, The Grange was squeezed between a church and an apartment building. It sat neglected and overlooked. In 2008, the building was restored, picked up, and moved to nearby St. Nicholas Park.

Child Labor

Hamilton said that if young children worked in factories, it would make them "more useful." This may sound bad in today's world, but he thought it would give kids a chance to earn money and help their families. He worked as a clerk when he was a teenager, and it was "the most useful of his education."

Shared Idea

On a trip to Europe, Jefferson noticed that the plows being used could be improved. When he got home, he designed a plow that was much more efficient. He chose not to **patent** the idea so that other farmers could use it for free.

On the Farm

Jefferson was a country boy, a Virginian. In those days, the United States was mostly an **agricultural** society. Jefferson wanted it to stay that way. He believed that farming was the natural way of life. People tied to the land kept "alive that sacred fire" of personal liberty. He believed that cities, on the other hand, were places of **corruption**. They were full of merchants who only cared about money. He called cities "great sores."

A farmer and his family harvesting in colonial America

A busy New York City street before Washington's inauguration at Federal Hall.

All Business

Hamilton was a city boy, a New Yorker. He didn't think cities were sores. In fact, he was sure they made the country healthier. Cities were centers of **commerce** and manufacturing. Businesses created and spread wealth. They attracted workers from other countries to America. Even farmers benefited from cities. They could sell crops there and buy cheap goods. Commerce made people energetic and inventive. A nation that grows things, makes things, and sells things is stronger than a country that doesn't do all three. In the long run, Hamilton's vision came true: America's economy became based more on **industry** than agriculture.

Government

In 1789, George Washington became president. He chose Hamilton as secretary of the treasury. Jefferson became **secretary of state**. It wasn't long before Hamilton and Jefferson began to clash. This is when the real rivalry between the two men began.

Hamilton wanted a strong central government. He thought it would be better for the nation. A loose collection of states almost lost the Revolution. They couldn't even collect **taxes** to pay their army. Hamilton wanted to expand the powers of the federal government. It should have the power to collect taxes, create an army, make treaties, and enforce laws. He was in favor of a powerful leader who would rule for life. He also believed decisions should be made by "landholders, merchants, and men of experience." He believed the common people "seldom judge or determine right."

This statue of Hamilton is in front of the Treasury Building.

Jefferson thought that Hamilton's ideas would lead to a **monarchy**. Hamilton's ideal leader was too powerful. The position would be the same as a king. States would not have a fair say in matters that affect them. Jefferson thought states should control their own fates. He believed that government should not trust a few people to represent the views of the whole country. The debate over the balance of state and federal powers continues today.

Washington and his cabinet: Henry Knox, Hamilton, Jefferson, and Edmund Randolph

1786 Rebellion

Ex-soldiers of the Revolution who wanted back pay started an uprising called Shay's Rebellion. Hamilton was against any attack on the national government. But Jefferson approved of the rebellion. He once wrote, "The tree of liberty must be refreshed from time to time with the blood of patriots and tyrants. It is its natural manure."

Striking a Balance

Hamilton believed that once leaders were elected into office, they should be allowed to serve "during good behavior." This meant that there would be no limit to the amount of time that they could be in office. James Madison called this an "elective monarchy."

The Issue of Slavery

On many issues, Hamilton and Jefferson were like night and day. One major example of this was slavery.

Jefferson owned about 200 enslaved people. But he said he opposed slavery. He thought it was **immoral** and hurt the Southern economy. Yet Jefferson never tried to end slavery. He didn't want to lose support of Southern slaveholders. There was also fear that if slaves were freed, war would follow. His solution? At some point in the future, he thought they should ship any freed enslaved people out of the country.

Many Founding Fathers owned slaves. This includes Jefferson, Washington, Patrick Henry, and James Madison. Washington wrote in his will that his slaves were to be freed upon his wife's death and left them money. Jefferson freed only a handful of his slaves.

Tools such as the wheel-driven lathe (left) and the two-man saw (above) were used during Monticello's construction.

Unliberated

Hamilton helped found the New-York Society for Promoting the Manumission [freeing] of Slaves and Protecting of Such of Them as Have Been or May Be Liberated. Surprisingly, some of the members of this group actually owned slaves. Hamilton tried to get those members to free their slaves, but they wouldn't.

Hamilton grew up in the West Indies. He witnessed slavery's brutality firsthand. He believed in **abolishing** slavery. During the Revolutionary War, Hamilton wanted enslaved people to fight the British. In exchange, they would be freed. Later, Hamilton helped start an anti-slavery group. He criticized people "who hold the bill of rights in one hand and a whip for affrighted slaves in the other." He meant slaveholders like Jefferson. They talked about protecting the rights of people, but they didn't think that those rights should apply to everybody.

Political Parties

Other politicians began to choose sides between Hamilton and Jefferson. Hamilton's followers were called Federalists. They were in favor of a strong central government. Jefferson led a group called the Democratic-Republicans. They preferred a government where the states held most of the power. The two parties clashed as much as their leaders.

Choosing a Home

In 1790, people began talking about the permanent capital of the United States. At the time, New York City was the home of the president and Congress. Most people thought it would stay there. They were even planning to build a new mansion for President Washington to live in. Hamilton loved having the capital in his hometown, but it wasn't everybody's top choice.

Jefferson didn't want the capital to stay in New York. It was too far from the South. A capital too far north would be more likely to reflect northern ideals. Jefferson proposed that the capital move to Virginia, along the Potomac River.

Washington put it up to a vote. Whichever location got the most votes would be the new capital. It looked like a majority of the politicians would vote for New York City. Jefferson was going to need help to get his way.

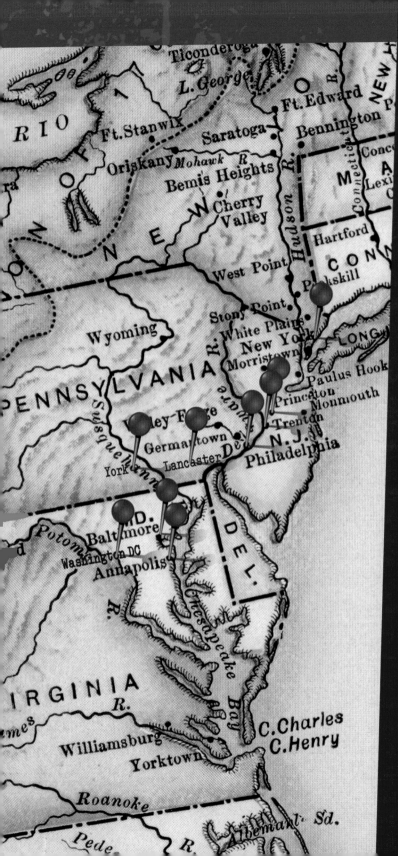

Chatterbox

Hamilton's wordy nature got on Jefferson's nerves. After one cabinet meeting, Jefferson wrote a note that said, "Hamilton made a jury speech of three quarters of an hour." The next day, after another meeting, Jefferson wrote, "Met again. Hamilton spoke again ¾ of an hour."

Roaming Capital

The United States capital has actually been moved among nine different cities. Most of the moves took place during the Revolutionary War. The capital had to move to stay safe from the British Army.

continental currency

Printing Money

Part of the reason why the Revolutionary War was fought was because the British imposed unfair taxes. Congress didn't want to anger the public by doing the same thing, so it decided to print more money to pay off the debt. This led to big problems later on.

Behind a Door

The Compromise of 1790 is also known as the "Dinner Table Bargain." Many people were upset that only three men made a decision that affected the entire country.

Money Matters

Some of the biggest battles that Hamilton and Jefferson fought were over money. Hamilton was in charge of the treasury. He had big plans to strengthen the economy of the United States. But Jefferson thought that some of his ideas tested the limits of Hamilton's power.

Round one was over debts. The United States owed a lot of money because of the Revolutionary War. Hamilton believed the federal government should assume the states' debts. That would help the country build credit. This was called the Assumption Bill.

Jefferson thought the plan was unfair. Some states had already paid what they owed. Why should those states have to help pay for the states that still owed money? As it turned out, most of the states that had already paid off their debts were in the South. So, Jefferson had an idea.

Jefferson invited Hamilton to dinner at his house. He also invited James Madison. Madison was a Democratic-Republican from Virginia who opposed Hamilton's debt plan. While they were there, the three men came up with a compromise. Madison and Jefferson would support Hamilton's debt plan. In return, Hamilton would support Jefferson's idea to move the U.S. capital to Virginia. Round one was a tie.

Assumption Bill

Copy 1   1 H 2 D 2. 1

Jan. 9, 1790 or 14th

REPORT

OF THE

Abr. Baldwin

SECRETARY of the TREASURY

TO THE

HOUSE of REPRESENTATIVES,

RELATIVE TO A PROVISION

FOR THE

SUPPORT

OF THE

PUBLIC CREDIT

OF THE

UNITED STATES,

IN CONFORMITY TO A RESOLUTION OF THE TWENTY-FIRST DAY OF
SEPTEMBER, 1789.

PRESENTED TO THE HOUSE ON THURSDAY THE 14th DAY OF JANUARY, 1790.

PUBLISHED BY ORDER OF THE HOUSE OF REPRESENTATIVES.

NEW-YORK:
PRINTED BY FRANCIS CHILDS AND JOHN SWAINE.
M,DCC,XC.

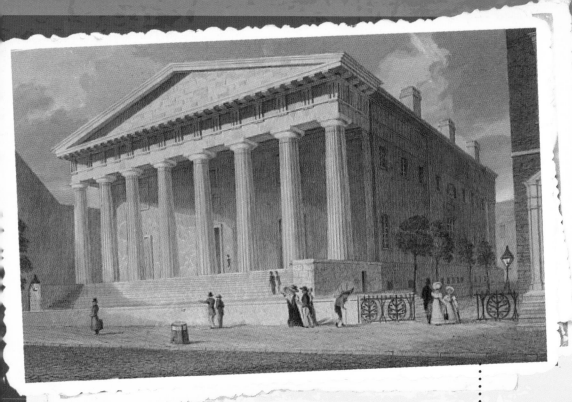

First Bank of the United States

Bank on It

Round two was fought over whether to create a national bank. Hamilton believed that a common bank with branches in each state would help the nation's economy. At the time, there was no national currency. Most people just traded goods and services. The nation couldn't collect taxes fairly without a **standard of value**. A bank that existed in all the states could create that. It would also be a place where the federal government could deposit its money or get loans.

On the other hand, Jefferson did not like the idea of a national bank. He argued that the Constitution doesn't mention a national bank, so it would be illegal. This was a "strict" reading of the Constitution. Hamilton used a "loose" reading. He claimed the Constitution gives the government powers not directly mentioned. The Constitution says the government can regulate commerce. A national bank is needed to do that.

Washington sided with Hamilton, and a national bank was formed. This round went to Hamilton.

High Price to Pay

Jefferson did all he could to stop the national bank. He even tried to punish any banker in Virginia who had anything to do with a central bank. Jefferson said that they would be "guilty of high treason and suffer death accordingly by the judgment of the state courts."

Buying Power

Jefferson didn't always practice what he preached when it came to interpreting the Constitution. In 1803, he purchased the Louisiana Territory from France. There was nothing in the Constitution that gave him the power to buy land. But, he did it anyway.

21

Tar-Nation

Angry whiskey-makers sometimes tarred and feathered tax collectors. They rubbed hot pine over victims and stuck feathers on them. It was painful and humiliating but not deadly.

Pardon Me

When the Whiskey Rebellion ended, 24 men were put on trial for high treason. This is a crime punishable by death. All except two men were found not guilty. President Washington later pardoned the two men who were convicted.

An Unpopular Law...

Jefferson and Hamilton continued to disagree on almost every decision they made. In 1791, Hamilton needed to find a way to pay off the debts that the United States owed from the Revolutionary War. He decided to place a tax on whiskey.

Whiskey-makers believed the tax would mostly affect small farmers. The farmers would often make whiskey with their leftover crops. This helped them make extra money. The tax felt unfair to them. For three years, protests remained peaceful. Then things turned violent. Five thousand angry rebels prepared to march on Pittsburgh. They believed that the new tax was no better than Great Britain's old taxes. Something needed to be done.

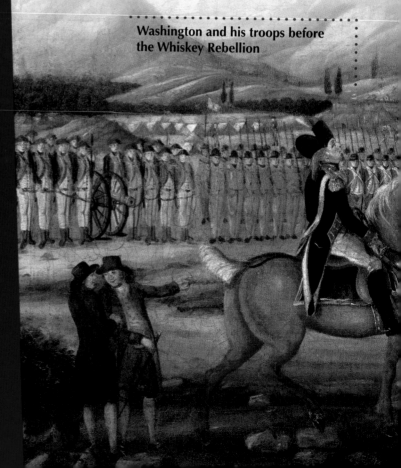

Washington and his troops before the Whiskey Rebellion

Hamilton helped lead over 13,000 troops to **suppress** what became known as the Whiskey Rebellion. He said even unpopular laws must be obeyed. "Shall the majority govern or be governed? Shall there be government or no government?"

At first, Jefferson said nothing about the tax. It was part of the deal he had made with Hamilton over dinner the year before. Later, he called the whiskey tax "infernal." He also thought it was wrong to use American troops against their own people. The tax was not repealed until 1802, when Jefferson was president.

Daniel Morgan commanded troops that stopped the rebellion.

Global Concerns

The French Revolution split France. On one side, you had the king and the noble class who helped America win its freedom. On the other side were the lower-class citizens who fought for democracy. This made it hard for Americans to choose a side to defend. They decided that it would be best to remain **neutral**. Then, in 1793 France went to war against Great Britain. This made it even harder for Americans to decide where they stood.

Rivals at War

Jefferson always thought highly of France. He thought even more of them after the French Revolution. It swept out the king and brought democracy to the country. Jefferson hated kings. Great Britain was a monarchy and a former enemy. Hamilton had once told Jefferson that Britain "is the most perfect government which ever existed." The thought of the United States as a monarchy scared Jefferson.

The French Revolution was a violent time for France.

Hamilton was pro-Britain. Its government was stable, and its economy was strong. Great Britain was America's main trading partner. It was in the best interests of the United States not to anger them. To Hamilton, the French Revolution was the bigger threat. Some freedom fighters threatened to take the revolution beyond France. If its violence spread to America, their new government could be thrown out as violently as France's had.

Thomas Jefferson was an ambassador to France.

The French Ask for Help

Edward Charles Genet was a French ambassador sent to the United States to create anti-British sentiment. He was trying to gain support for the French Revolution. His goal was to find a base from which **privateers** could attack British ships. However, Washington wanted to stay out of the war and denied Genet any help.

Vive La France!

Jefferson loved all things French. Many parts of Monticello have a distinct French influence. For example, the dome on the top of Jefferson's famous home is modeled after the Hotel de Salm. This was a palace in France that he particularly liked.

Rock Bottom

When Hamilton spoke publicly in favor of the Jay Treaty in New York City, some members of the crowd threw rocks at him. One stone hit him in the head. Hamilton joked with the mob, "If you use such knock-down arguments, I must retire."

Taking Freedom

The Sedition Act was one of four acts passed by the Federalists in 1798 that became known as the Alien and Sedition Acts. They were used to suppress the freedoms of Americans who didn't agree with government. These acts turned out to be the downfall of Adams's presidency.

Choosing Sides

The British upset Americans by placing **tariffs** and trade restrictions on their goods. Matters got worse when the British captured U.S. ships that were sailing to French ports.

Democratic-Republicans wanted to fight Britain. Hamilton tried to avoid conflict. In 1794, he helped work out a deal called the Jay Treaty. The treaty kept America out of war. It also limited their trade rights and made them repay pre-revolutionary debts. Jefferson said it was a "monument to folly." He believed Hamilton gave up too much to the British in an attempt to avoid war.

Speechless

France was also upset about the Jay Treaty and began to capture U.S. ships in 1798. President John Adams was ready to fight. Talk of war with France scared Democratic-Republicans. They attacked the government in the newspapers. The Federalists decided to keep their rivals quiet. They passed the Sedition Act in 1798. The act made it illegal to "write, print, or publish" anything opposing the U.S. government. Jefferson tried to get states to overturn the act. He said the law went against freedom of speech. Hamilton argued that states could not overturn a federal law. The Sedition Act stuck.

Alien and Sedition Law

An Act

Supplementary to, and to amend the act, intituled, " An act to establish an uniform rule of naturalization; and to repeal the act heretofore passed on that subject."

Sect. 1. BE it enacted by the Senate and House of Representatives of the United States of America, in Congress assembled, That no alien shall be admitted to become a citizen of the United States, or of any state, unless in the manner prescribed by the act, intituled " An act to establish an uniform rule of naturalization ; and to repeal the act heretofore passed on that subject," he shall have declared his intention to become a citizen of the United States, five years, at least, before his admission, and shall, at the time of his application to be admitted, declare and prove, to the satisfaction of the court having jurisdiction in the case, that he has resided within the United States fourteen years, at least, and within the state or territory where, or for which such court is at the time held, five years, at least, besides conforming to the other declarations, renunciations and proofs, by the said act required, any thing therein to the contrary hereof notwithstanding : *Provided,* That any alien, who was residing within the limits, and under the jurisdiction of the United States, before the twenty-ninth day of January, one thousand seven hundred and ninety-five, may, within one year after the passing of this act—and any alien who shall have made the declaration of his intention to become a citizen of the United States, in conformity to the provisions of the act, intituled " An act to establish an uniform rule of naturalization, and to repeal the act heretofore passed on that subject," may, within four years after having made the declaration aforesaid, be admitted to become a citizen, in the manner prescribed by the said act, upon his making proof that he has resided five years, at least, within the limits, and under the jurisdiction of the United States : *And provided also,* That no alien, who shall be a native, citizen, denizen or subject of any nation or state with whom the United States shall be at war, at the time of his application, shall be then admitted to become a citizen of the United States.

Sec. 2. *And be it further enacted,* That it shall be the duty of the clerk, or other recording officer of the court before whom a declaration has been, or shall be made, by any alien, of his intention to become a citizen of the United States, to certify and transmit to the office of the Secretary of State of the United States, to be there filed and recorded, an abstract of such declaration, in which, when hereafter made, shall be a suitable description of the name, age, nation, residence and occupation, for the time being, of the alien; such certificate to be made in all cases, where the declaration has been or shall be made, before the passing of this act, within three months thereafter ; and in all other cases within two months after the declaration shall be received by the court : And in all cases hereafter arising, there shall be paid to the clerk, or recording officer as aforesaid, to defray the expense of such abstract and certificate, a fee of two dollars ; and the clerk or officer to whom such fee shall be paid or tendered, who shall refuse or neglect to make and certify an abstract, as aforesaid, shall forfeit and pay the sum of ten dollars.

Sec. 3. *And be it further enacted,* That in all cases of naturalization heretofore permitted or which shall be permitted, under the laws of the United States, a certificate shall be made to, and filed in the office of the Secretary of State, containing a copy of the record respecting the alien, and the decree or order of admission by the court before whom the proceedings thereto have been, or shall be had : And it shall be the duty of the clerk or other recording officer of such court, to make and transmit such certificate, in all cases which have already occurred, within three months after the passing of this act ; and in all future cases, within two months from and after the naturalization of an alien shall be granted by any court competent thereto : And in all future cases there shall be paid to such clerk or recording officer the sum of two dollars, as a fee for such certificate, before the naturalization prayed for, shall be allowed : And the clerk or recording officer, whose duty it shall be to make and transmit the certificate aforesaid, who shall be convicted of a wilful neglect therein, shall forfeit and pay the sum of ten dollars for each and every offence.

Sect. 4. *And be it further enacted,* That all white persons, aliens, (accredited foreign ministers, consuls, or agents, their families and domestics excepted) who, after the passing of this act, shall continue to reside, or who shall arrive, or come to reside in any port or place within the territory of the United States, shall be reported, if free, and of the age of twenty-one years, by themselves, or being under the age of twenty-one years, or holden in service by their parent, guardian, master or mistress in whose care they shall be, to the clerk of the district court of the district, if living within ten miles of the port or place in which their residence or arrival shall be and otherwise, to the collector of such port or place, or some officer or other person nearest thereto, who shall be authorized by the President of the United States to register aliens : And a report, as aforesaid, shall be made in all cases of residence, within six months from and after the passing of this act, and in all after cases, within forty-eight hours after the first arrival or coming into the territory of the United States, and shall ascertain the sex, place of birth, age, nation, place of allegiance or citizenship, condition or occupation, and place of actual or intended residence within the United States, of the alien or aliens reported, and by whom the report is made. And it shall be the duty of the clerk, or other officer, or person, authorized, who shall receive such report, to record the same in a book to be kept for that purpose, and to grant to the person making the report, and to each individual concerned therein, whenever required, a certificate of such report and registry and whenever such report and registry shall be made, to, and by any officer or person authorized, as aforesaid, other than the clerk of the district court, it shall be the duty of such officer or person, to certify and transmit, within three months thereafter, a transcript of such registry, to the said clerk of the district court of the district in which the same shall happen ; who shall file the same in his office, and shall enter and transcribe the same in a book to be kept by him for that purpose. And the clerk, officer or other person authorized to register aliens, shall be entitled to receive, for each report and registry of one individual or family of individuals, the sum of fifty cents, and for every certificate of a report and registry, the sum of fifty cents, to be paid by the person making or requiring the same, respectively. And the clerk of the district court, to whom a return of such registry shall have been made, as aforesaid, and the successor of such clerk, ... thorized to register aliens, who .....

	Thomas Jefferson of Virginia	Aaron Burr New York	John Adams Massachusetts	Charles Cotesworth Pinckney of South Carolina	John Jay New York
New Hampshire			6	6	
Massachusetts			16	16	
Rhode Island			4	3	1
Connecticut			9	9	
Vermont			4	4	
New York	12	12			
New Jersey			7	7	
Pennsylvania	8	8	7	7	
Delaware			3	3	
Maryland	5	5	5	5	
Virginia	21	21			
Kentucky	4	4			
North Carolina	8	8	4	4	
Tennessee	3	3			
South Carolina	8	8			
Georgia	4	4			
	73	73	65	64	1

This document shows the tally of electoral votes for the 1800 presidential election.

Cutting Losses

When Jefferson ran for president in 1796, Hamilton worked against his election. He helped John Adams win. It wasn't a complete loss for Jefferson, though— he became vice president.

Jefferson ran for president again in 1800. This time he beat Adams but tied with Aaron Burr. Hamilton had feuded with Burr more than he had with Jefferson. He called Burr "One of the most unprincipled men in the United States." At least Jefferson had principles. It was up to the House of Representatives to decide the winner. Hamilton talked House members into voting for Jefferson.

Rivals at Rest

Jefferson and Hamilton were both passionate about the new country. They fought for what they believed in. The election of 1800 proved that these men could put aside personal differences for the sake of the country. Both men believed in the promise of the United States and wanted it to succeed. It wasn't one man or the other who the country took after. Reflections of both men can be seen in the country today. Both men set a young country on the path to greatness.

Thomas Jefferson

Faint Praise

In a dig at Burr, Hamilton (sort of) praised Burr's opponent, Jefferson. "There is no doubt that upon every **virtuous** and **prudent** calculation, Jefferson is to be preferred. He is by far not so dangerous a man."

Handing Over the Keys

The election of 1800 marked the first transfer of political power in U.S. history. People were afraid that this would lead to war. Luckily, it turned out to be a peaceful transition. Jefferson called for peace in his inaugural speech. He said, "We are all Republicans, we are all Federalists."

Glossary

abolishing—formally putting an end to

agricultural—related to farming or raising livestock

commerce—the buying and selling of goods in a country or between countries

corruption—not doing what is moral or considered correct in society

debt—something that is owed

Founding Fathers—the people who were most involved in creating the United States

immoral—not good or right

industry—businesses that work in manufacturing

legacy—anything handed down from the past to future generations

monarchy—a government headed by a single person, such as a king

neutral—not taking one side or the other in a conflict

patent—protect with a trademark to establish ownership rights

privateers—private citizens given permission by a government to attack foreign ships

profound—having deep meaning or insight

prudent—showing thoughtfulness

rivalries—competitions; disagreements

secretary of state—a member of the president's cabinet who gives advice on foreign policy

secretary of the treasury—a member of the president's cabinet who gives advice on the nation's financial matters

standard of value—an agreed upon value for goods and services based on a common unit of exchange (such as a dollar)

suppress—to forcibly stop something from happening

tariffs—taxes

taxes—the money a government collects from citizens and businesses to help run the government

virtuous—making good moral decisions

Index

Your Turn!

Look closely at the continental currency. Also look at some current bills. What features or symbols do you find on currency today? What makes the colonial currency different from the currency of today? Take elements from the colonial money and from today's currency to design a new look for American money. Provide an explanation of the elements that you include and why you chose them. Create at least three different bills.